A Little Book of
Quirky Poems

Samantha Weber

BookLeaf
Publishing

India | USA | UK

Presentation by *BookLeaf Publishing*

Web: www.bookleafpub.com

E-mail: info@bookleafpub.com

ISBN: 9789360947361

First edition 2024

*For those who experience human emotions,
and who have allowed me to do the same
without guilt.*

ACKNOWLEDGEMENT

I'd like to acknowledge my parents, Linda and Philip Weber, who have always supported me in all of my half-baked endeavors, and who have never stifled my creativity (even if, more often than not, my creative outlets ended in disaster).

PREFACE

When I saw this writing opportunity pop up on my Instagram feed, I figured that it was the universe's way of telling me that I should finally take a risk and publish some of my work. Granted, most of my poems are hastily written or intended to be recorded as songs, but there are still some fun concepts enclosed within this book. I never thought I would pursue a career in writing, and I still don't, but the idea that I could have a book with my name on it as a high-schooler? That sounded pretty sweet. Some of these poems are years old, and some were written an hour before the final book was due. The emotional weight of my work ranges drastically, from super depressing to mildly funny, but I hope that my words speak to someone out there.

Story of a Loser

Who am I
I say to the mirror with tears in my eyes
The voices in my head harass me with their
words
The very same ones that make me feel hurt
My journey is long
My story ain't pretty
But listen long enough,
And surely you'll find it to be worthy.

I come from a land I will never return to
I developed in the womb of someone I will
likely never know
I'd play alone with the blocks at preschool
I'd play by myself in the snow.

I found comfort in the oddities- the subtleties-
the nonconformities
I realized I had a voice stronger than the tiny
body given to me
As I hung from my bars I jumped for once and
guess what I reached the stars
I got so high it felt so inspiring I just sat there in
awe
My words made me feel alive

Like happiness was finally within reach

Until the others understood that my weakness
was their strength.

They beat me down and broke me
My soul damn nearly left me
I hang with my demons wishing I was hanging
with my body
As I cried tears and tasted blood I felt so fucking
lonely
Medications observations and all the shit that
they sold to me

I felt so numb
My bullies laughed at me constantly
I felt so dumb
For believing I could be happy

There are still these moments
They remind me of the loneliness
They make me remember too much of the pain
that I hide desperately
The past just keeps coming back to haunt this
old soul mercilessly

From a young age I was different
It's just another fact
Like how the Earth goes around the Sun

But what happens when the Sun turns its back?
I was born with too much of this, but not enough
of that

But maybe… just maybe... for once I'm a
balanced act.

song about space pt. 1

I find myself floating, here in outer space.
So far away, no one knows my face.
Out here all alone, no way to go home
Trapped at the edge of the galaxy
Exiled by all the mockery

My dreams transformed into beings that scared
me
Here in outer space, I exist without humanity
Planets in the distance are boasting their stars.
How I wish it were possible to combine their
light with ours.
To be able to harness their powers would be to
prolong the hours
With which I can exist at peace, laying under
fiery meteor showers.

To be Happy

I had a revelation today…
To explain it in the best way, imagine one of those sieves
I used to steal them for crafts, a happy little thief.
Most people contain in their head
A flower pot, a bowl, or a vessel instead
Something to contain what keeps them from tossing in their bed.

On the other hand there are people like me
Who are cursed to be creative
Forced to find other means
To be able to carry contentedness
To hold it close and use it to shield from negativity
Capable of escaping, the happiness musn't be

Broken I remain until the day of the rapture
In place of a sturdy receptacle
I have only one filled with fractures
A sort of hole-y, leaky, insufficient thing
A colander, a sieve, incapable of capture.

For The Ones Who Couldn't Make It

Frankly I must say that the fact that I am still
here truly baffles me
Playfully I can do what I may but the point still
stands that my story is one of dismay
Ultimately I am able only to extend an invisible
hand to those who are left lonely
Hopefully someday, we can all live in some
semblance of harmony.

song about space pt. 2

Without a will
Without a dream
This is the only way to keep my hands clean.

Alone with my thoughts, I'm trapped in my
head.
I grasp myself as I lay cold in bed.
I belong on the floor.
Self-damnation be true.
Up again to get the door.
Slam it shut, keep out the crew.
Throw out the key.
Leave it floating out there, for an indeterminate
infinity.

I'm floating in a galaxy
A prison of my own creation.
Drowning in a gigantic sea.
Trying to survive in uncharted territory.
Trudging through, no choice but to ignore
uncertainty.
The world pushes me to its edge, plunging me
into some sick, twisted odyssey.

A Poem Long Enough to Be a Song: Praise for the True but Wronged.

This is for all the people who were born alone
Helpless and unable
No blankets, kisses, or homes

This is for the misfits hiding in the shadows
Scared of being burnt by the sharp tongues of
others
Sentenced to remain chained within their
hallows

This is for everyone who has been hurt or
broken
Left damaged and bruised
Whose mirrors showed only a face way sullen

This is for the victims of all types of ruse
The targets the fakers the creators and the
players
Those whose experiences can be described only
as abuse

This is for the straw that broke the camel's back

The one minor comment that really made me
crack

All the hate and the flack
All the bull and the crap

This is for the hypocrisy
The mockery
The stupidity
The lack of unity
For everything you fired at me
I will fire straight back at you with fury

Because this is for the cut down
This is for the used
This is for the battered
The numb
And the perused

For the insane not given no chance to change
For the skeletons in my closet so neatly arranged

For the 5 years of BS I had to go through
Someone always had it worse
Don't I know it to be true
But

What about the taunting
The musings

The blocking

The gaslighting
The firefighting
The thunder and the lightning

I'm going psycho now
Now I'm really seeing ghosts
But they aren't random
They are people I know

For all the times I tried to make it right
I tried to kneel in what had to be a fight
For every minute I cried myself red
For every morning I woke up in a sweat soaked
bed

To all the bullies and the asses
The bitches itching to resort to harassment
The cowards who sat and covered their eyes
Scared of what would happen

I ask that you reflect
I hope you get to feel like a damn reject
With my scars in the air
I look up to the stars and I stare
I thank whatever the hell is out there
That I found my way through that toxic
laissez-faire

But hey, that's just me
An average Jane Doe
Nobody to love
Nothing to show

So here is my cry
For the ridiculed and mangled
The people who want to die
The oppressed
The depressed
The lonely
The fighters

I believe in you
Broken but true
Grounded and sure
Desired not endured

This is for the bullied
The broken
The bruised

The battered
The tattered
The woke
And the used

For all the wronged out there

I believe in you

Of Bugs

I saw a sad wasp today
Its wings were broken
Its antennae in disarray.

Wasps are the villains
That's what we are taught
Kill them by the millions
Useful, they are not.

I took the cup and dropped it on the beast
With a plastic plop, the wasp accepts its defeat
Be glad I am not the hunter. Be glad, little wasp,
that you I cannot eat.

Graciously beg for mercy
From within your see-through cage
It's rare for the predator to be apt at business so
dirty

Dealing with a fly is quick and easy
A flick of the wrist and its offers are ceased.
Dealing with a wasp, with reputations of
cunning
Danger is inevitable. Impossibilities are
becoming.

As the wasp's world goes blurry
I watch its head fall to peace
For I am the giant who has given it mercy.

song about space pt. 3

I'm just a girl, floating in outer space.
I have done nothing, but I feel so out of place.
Making myself crazy, I am feeling so down.

Look in the mirror. Take off your crown.
When all's said and done, maybe you are the
clown.
Jesters call me names. They bring me no fame.
Glory be… well, I guess, quite boring.

Guess that ship has sailed
One way or another, make sure I don't fail.

In pain, I'm insane, showering and cowering,
crying while shivering under water droplets.
However I got here, I cannot leave. And so I
remain, an astronaut in space
Don't know if I am lost…
But I am so flagrantly out of place.

Hush my darling

Hush my darling
Sleep sound and wake not
For the call of the starling
Is what I've set out to stop

Rest at peace, dreaming of me
Imagining our reality soon to be

Brown eyes and brown hair
Bushy brows and hands bare
I'm watching you sleep, happily unaware

My dear darling,
Hush your innocent mind
Know of my intentions
To fulfill you, who speaks of me so kind

Of Grass

Generic and underwhelming
Blades of grass can be very showing
Animals trekking leave them disturbed
Through bushes and dirt and piles of burrs

Stay quiet and watch the grass sing
As it swishes to and fro
Itching to expose secrets
Of a world yet to be known

Look closely and expose more to see
Colors change based on soil range
The grass chooses its home strategically
There it resides, no arms, no eyes.
Watching the world go 'round
Witness to every new lie.

Out of Reach

Imagine if I could jump super-duper high
Mama, look at me, I'm gonna fly
I'll be bigger than our house someday
Strong enough to make my own way
I'll be able to do it all, mama
Protect us all from harm.

Promises I've made
Debts I've had to pay
Life throws at me what it may.

I ain't tall enough for creating diffs
I'd be the pointless top of the pyramid
Climbed all that way just to have a chance to
pray
For a better life that I been working towards
Even though in my face be slamming all the
doors
Just keep going just keep moving don't let
anyone know you're using–
Keep on jumpin' keep on grinding keep your
head on your shoulders, the prize I be eyeballin'
Don't stop don't stall don't let go of it all don't
let your drive leave ya, ain't no angels callin'

The bar keeps moving up and up
You wanna touch it? That still ain't enough.
It's outta reach for real this time.
Don't matter how you spent your time.
Learning to scale a wall, making a fence to
climb.
We playin' these games, like they weren't just
created in our minds.

Don't

Don't tell me that I am like an angel with broken
wings
Washed up and useless, just a pretty, sad, little
thing.
Don't call me the name that I outgrew long ago
Condemning me for being someone I already
don't know.
Don't scold me for making do with what I was
given
Accuse me of not being smart enough to earn
some random ribbon.
Don't look me in the eyes and tell me you've
loved me all this time
Insulting this way only leave splotches on both
our minds.
Don't text me when you're sad and alone at
nighttime
You already know you threw away what I was
willing to give a lifetime.

Nonsensical

Letters
Flighty feathers
Telling to tether
Pandas passing poor petters
Actually acting as an accreditor
Scrutinizing several sunny sandy secondary
subletters
Goons gone golfing gonna grapple go getters

Ah, that's better.
Let's forget the past and stand grown.

Wrong Way

22

Driving to the store on the I-95
Blinkers are on while I'm reading the signs
Following my GPS, keeping track of the line
Blaring my music and forgetting the time
How I love driving, in the middle of the night.

Insanity

Sirius Serious,

There they're.
It's its
Not knot
Fair fare

You ewe
Look luck
So sew
Bare bear

Should shooed
Sell cell
Your you're
Hair hare

Try tri
And end
Know no
Where wear

For four
Some sum
Sun son

Tear tare

Break brake
Right write
See sea
Pear pair

Young

I'm in love with this guy and he has the most
beautiful eyes
They glisten wherever they are, under
fluorescents, under the Texan stars
I'm in love with his hair, scruffy and going bare
His smile that warms me from the inside without
fail

... And Stupid

Making up scenarios in my head
The last thing I think about before going to bed
I hear his laugh in the corner of my room
I see his glistening smile and I swoon

Superglue

I wonder if Superman ever tried to superglue his
cracks
My brother had this action figure, and so I tested
that fact.
His hand had crumbled away from years of
nonstop play
The hero's neck had loosened from seemingly
endless use.

I went to the drawer in the kitchen next to the
spoons
I picked out the superglue and told Superman
he'd be better soon
Even alien beings only susceptible to kryptonite
need to heal sometimes.

9 789360 947361